Grammaropolis
PRESENTS

Jake the Adjective

Written by Coert Voorhees
Illustrations by Powerhouse Animation

Meet the Parts of Speech

I name a specific person, place, thing, or idea. It's a big responsibility, naming things— a responsibility that requires a certain attention to detail.

Nelson the Noun

Some people say I'm all over the place. Some people call me a ball of energy. I take that as a compliment, because I just like to go, go, go!

Vinny the Action Verb

I take the place of one or more Nouns or Pronouns. I always want the Noun's job, and I hang out with the Verb and Adjective.

Roger the Pronoun

I'm perfectly happy to link Nouns and Pronouns with the appropriate Adjectives, but it's not like I'm going to expend a lot of energy doing so.

Lucy the Linking Verb

I modify a Noun or Pronoun. I tell what kind, which one, how many, or how much. I pride myself on being the most artistic of the parts of speech.

Jake the Adjective

Gather 'round everybody and let's have ourselves a wonderful time. I just love bringing words and groups of words together, don't you?

Connie the Conjunction

I modify a Verb, Adjective, or other Adverb. I tell how, when, where, to what extent, and under what condition. I often end in –ly, but I don't have to.

Benny the Adverb

I express emotion!! Yep, I'm always here, always ready with my commas and exclamation points, just in case.

Izzy the Interjection

They call me Preposition because I'm pre-positioned. I'm first. At the front. Before every other word in the phrase? Got it?

Li'l Pete the Preposition

I am a chameleon. A spy. An undercover operative. I infiltrate the sentence and act as whatever part of speech suits me.

Slang

JAKE THE ADJECTIVE

Like all adjectives, Jake dreamed in color.

RED COBALT

Jade gold lavender

3

Boddington had been the nicest adjective in Grammaropolis, but one day he became mean. Nobody knew why.

Everything is grey and brown. And more grey.

There was no time to waste. Jake quickly restored the colors.

So Jake used adjectives of size to modify them back.

It's small again. Petite, even.

Meow.

MODIFYING A NOUN

My father is a brave man.

MODIFYING A PRONOUN

He is brave.

WHAT KIND
I only wear *purple* shoes on Tuesdays.

WHICH ONE
My cousin always sits in the *front* row.

HOW MUCH
(QUANTITY)
Please give me *more* chocolate.

HOW MANY
(AMOUNT)
I would like *seven* chocolate bars.

POSSESSIVE ADJECTIVES

A **possessive adjective** modifies a noun, showing possession or ownership.

That is **my** box of cereal!

Your dog accidentally ate **his** homework.

EXAMPLES

my
Your
his

DEMONSTRATIVE ADJECTIVES

A demonstrative adjective shows whether the noun it modifies is singular or plural and whether it is near or far.

I want **this** cake instead of **that** cake over there.

Billy is about to throw **these** shoes at **those** people across the street.

EXAMPLES

this
that
these
those

INTERROGATIVE ADJECTIVES

An interrogative adjective modifies a noun and is used to ask a question.

Which cars are the most awesome?

What dessert do you like most?

EXAMPLES:

Which

What

COMPARATIVE ADJECTIVES

A comparative adjective is used to make a comparison between two nouns or pronouns.

This tree is taller than that one.

He is louder than she is.

EXAMPLES

taller
louder

SUPERLATIVE ADJECTIVES

A **superlative adjective** describes the extreme quality of something. It is used when talking about three or more nouns or pronouns.

That tree is the **tallest** tree in the forest.

He is the **loudest** member of our family.

EXAMPLES

tallest
loudest

ARTICLES
(BABY ADJECTIVES)

The articles (a, an, and the) are the most frequently used adjectives. A and an are known as indefinite articles because they refer to a general noun (one that is not defined). The is a definite article because it refers to a specifc noun.

I think watching a movie is more fun than eating an artichoke.

I studied so hard for the test yesterday.

EXAMPLES

a
an
the

www.ingramcontent.com/pod-product-compliance
Lightning Source LLC
LaVergne TN
LVHW071213200326
834410LV00018B/573